Affiliate Marketing for Beginners

Tips and Tools to get started.

Introduction:

If you're interested in making money online, learning how to do affiliate marketing is a great way to get started.

But if you're new to the world of affiliate marketing, it can be challenging. That's where our new book comes in.

With step-by-step instructions and easy-to-follow examples, we'll walk you through everything you need to know to get started with affiliate marketing.

From choosing the right products to promote to creating content that converts, we'll cover a lot of topics for you to get started.

So whether you're looking to make a little extra income on the side or build a full-time business, our affiliate marketing for beginners book is the perfect place to start.

FREE RESOURCES:

*Free Membership to our Affiliate Marketing Training and Resource Platform
https://www.pastordre.com/wealthyaffiliate

Join our Affiliate Marketing platform of over 2.1 million members – Here is what comes with your FREE membership:

- A free website and blog
- 5 Affiliate Marketing bootcamp videos
- 30 Free keyword searches
- 5 Lessons of our Core Certification Course
- 50 Training Modules

I am an affiliate of this platform, so if you decide to upgrade your membership, I will get a commission. Upgrading is not necessary to receive FREE access to the above-mentioned goodies.

*FREE website and blog –
https://PastorDre.com/siterubix

*Social Media Automation Tool – Paid Tool
https://pastordre.com/automation

*Indicates that I am an affiliate of that platform.

Download 3 FREE Chapters Of an Audio Sample

3 Free Chapters to get you started on your affiliate marketing journey.

Table of Contents

Chapter 1 - Introduction to Affiliate Marketing

- What is Affiliate Marketing?
- How does Affiliate Marketing work?
- Why is Affiliate Marketing a good option for beginners?

Chapter 2 - Finding the Right Affiliate Program

- Choosing the Right Niche.
- Researching different Affiliate Programs.
- Finding the Right Fit for Your Website or Blog.

Chapter 3 - Build a Website or Blog

- Why having a website or blog is important for Affiliate Marketing.
- Choosing the right platform and domain name for Affiliate Marketing.
- Designing and building your site for Affiliate Marketing.

Chapter 4 - Creating Quality Content

- Why Creating Quality Content is Essential for Affiliate Marketing.
- Types of content that work best for affiliate marketing.
- Tips for creating engaging content that drives traffic and conversions.

Chapter 5 - Build an Email List

- Why Building an email list is Important for Affiliate Marketing.
- How to build an email list from scratch.
- Email marketing strategies for Affiliate Marketers.

Chapter 6 - Promoting Your Affiliate Links

- How to promote your Affiliate Links Effectively.
- Using Social Media to Promote your Affiliate Links.
- Other Ways to Promote Your Affiliate Links.

Chapter 7 - Tracking your Results.

- Why tracking your results is important for affiliate marketing.
- How to track your results using analytics tools.
- Analyzing your results and making adjustments.

Chapter 8 - Tips for Success

- Common mistakes to avoid in affiliate marketing.
- Tips for staying motivated and avoiding burnout.
- How to scale your affiliate marketing business.

Chapter 9 - Next Steps and Resources

- Where to go for more information and support.
- Tools and Resources for Affiliate Marketers.
- Next Steps for building a successful affiliate marketing business.

Chapter 10 - Legal and Ethical Considerations

- Understanding and Complying with FTC guidelines.
- How to disclose Affiliate Relationships Properly.
- Know Your Rights and Responsibilities as an Affiliate Marketer.

Resource Section

Chapter 1 – Introduction to Affiliate Marketing

- What is Affiliate Marketing?
- How does Affiliate Marketing work?
- Why is Affiliate Marketing a good option for beginners?

What is Affiliate Marketing?

Affiliate marketing is a type of marketing where a business rewards an affiliate for each customer or sale that is brought to their website through the affiliate's marketing efforts. This is a way for businesses to market their products or services through affiliates who have their own audience.

To put it simply, affiliate marketing is like a referral program. When someone recommends a product or service to a friend, they are essentially acting as an affiliate. In affiliate marketing, the affiliate is rewarded for their recommendation with a commission.

For example, let's say that you have a blog about fitness and health. You partner with a fitness company to become an affiliate. You promote their products on your blog, and if someone clicks on a link and purchases a product, you receive a commission.

Affiliate marketing is a win-win situation for both the business and the affiliate. The business gets exposure and sales, while the affiliate gets rewarded for their marketing efforts. It is a low-cost and low-risk way for businesses to advertise their products, and for affiliates to make money online.

How does affiliate marketing work?

Affiliate marketing is a performance-based marketing strategy in which an advertiser pays a commission to an affiliate for each sale or lead generated through their referral. The affiliate earns a commission for promoting the advertiser's products or services to their audience.

Here's a step-by-step breakdown of how affiliate marketing works:

1. The advertiser creates an affiliate program: The advertiser, also known as the merchant, creates an affiliate program and provides affiliates with a unique link to their website or product.

2. The affiliate promotes the advertiser's products: The affiliate, also known as the publisher, promotes the advertiser's products or services through various marketing channels

such as social media, email marketing, blogs, and websites.

3. The customer clicks on the affiliate link: When a customer clicks on the affiliate's unique link, they are redirected to the advertiser's website.

4. The customer makes a purchase: If the customer makes a purchase on the advertiser's website, the affiliate earns a commission.

5. The advertiser tracks and pays commissions: The advertiser tracks the referral made by the affiliate and pays them a commission for each sale or lead generated.

Affiliate marketing provides a win-win situation for both the advertiser and the affiliate. The advertiser benefits from increased exposure and sales, while the affiliate earns a commission for promoting the advertiser's products or services.

In order to be successful in affiliate marketing, it's important for affiliates to carefully select products and services that align with their audience's needs and interests.

It's also important to build trust with their audience and be transparent about their relationship with the advertiser.

Now that you have a basic understanding of how affiliate marketing works, it's time to dive deeper into the strategies and techniques that can help you succeed as an affiliate marketer.

In the following chapters, we'll explore topics like finding the right affiliate programs, promoting products effectively, and optimizing your affiliate marketing efforts for maximum success.

Why is Affiliate Marketing a Good option for Beginners?

Affiliate marketing is a great way for beginners to get started with online marketing. Here are a few reasons why:

1. Low startup costs: Affiliate marketing is a relatively low-cost business to start up. You don't need to create your own products or invest in inventory, so there are no upfront costs to worry about.

2. No need for a website: Although having a website can make it easier to promote products, it's not necessary for affiliate marketing. You can promote products through social media, email marketing, and other channels.

3. Flexibility: Affiliate marketing allows you to work from anywhere and on your own schedule. You don't need to worry about commuting or working set hours, so you can fit it around your other commitments.

4. No customer support: As an affiliate marketer, you're not responsible for customer support or dealing with returns and refunds. This means you can focus on promoting products and earning commissions.

5. High earning potential: Affiliate marketing can be a highly profitable business if done right. With the right strategy and products, you can earn a significant income without having to invest much time or money.

Overall, affiliate marketing is a great option for beginners who are looking to get started with online marketing. With low startup costs, flexibility, and high earning potential, it's a great way to build a successful business without having to invest a lot of time or money up front.

Chapter 2 – Finding the Right Affiliate Program

- Choosing the Right Niche
- Researching different Affiliate Programs
- Finding the Right Fit for Your Website or Blog

Choosing the right niche

Choosing the right niche is one of the most important decisions you'll make as an affiliate marketer. Your niche will determine who your target audience is, what topics you'll cover, and what products you'll promote. So how do you choose the right niche? Here are some tips:

1. Choose a niche that you're passionate about

If you're not interested in your niche, it will be hard to create content that resonates with your audience. So choose a niche that you're passionate about and that you know well. This will make it easier to create high-quality content that your audience will love.

2. Research your niche

Before you commit to a niche, do some research. Look at what other affiliate marketers are doing in your niche. What products are they promoting? What topics are they covering?

This will give you an idea of what's working and what's not in your niche. You can also use tools like Google Trends and Keyword Planner to see what people are searching for in your niche.

3. Choose a niche with high demand

You want to choose a niche that has a high demand for products and information.

This means that people are actively searching for solutions to problems in your niche. This will make it easier to promote products and to get traffic to your website.

4. Choose a niche with low competition

At the same time, you don't want to choose a niche that's too competitive.

If there are already a lot of established affiliate marketers in your niche, it will be harder for you to get noticed.

So choose a niche with moderate to low competition.

5. Choose a niche with high commission rates

Finally, you want to choose a niche with high commission rates. This means that you'll earn a higher percentage of each sale. Look for products in your niche that have high commission rates and that are in demand.

By following these tips, you'll be able to choose the right niche. Remember, the key is to choose a niche that you're passionate about, that has high demand and low competition, and that offers high commission rates. Once you've chosen your niche, you can start creating content and promoting products to your audience.

Researching Different Affiliate Programs

Now that you understand the basics of affiliate marketing, it's time to start exploring the different affiliate programs available to you. But with so many programs out there, how do you know which ones are right for your business? Here are some tips on how to research different affiliate programs and choose the right ones for you:

1. Start with a niche: The first step in finding the right affiliate programs is to focus on your niche. What products or services are you promoting?

Look for programs that are relevant to your niche, as these will be the most effective in converting your traffic into sales.

2. Check the commission rates: Commission rates can vary widely among different programs, so it's important to check them carefully.

Look for programs that offer a fair commission rate, but also keep in mind that the payout structure can vary as well. Some programs pay out a percentage of the sale, while others pay a flat fee per sale.

3. Look for quality products: It's important to promote products that are of high quality and that you believe in. Look for programs that offer products or services that you would use yourself, and that you think your audience would be interested in.

4. Consider the cookie length: The cookie length is the amount of time that a customer has to make a purchase after clicking on your affiliate link. Look for programs with longer cookie lengths, as this will give you a better chance of earning commissions on future purchases.

5. Check the program's reputation: Before signing up for any affiliate program, do some research on the company.

Look for reviews and testimonials from other affiliates to see if the program is reputable and has a good track record.

6. Look for support: Finally, consider the level of support that the program offers. Do they provide marketing materials and other resources to help you promote their products? Do they have a dedicated support team to help you with any questions or issues that may arise?

By taking the time to research different affiliate programs and choosing the right ones for your business, you can maximize your earning potential and build a successful affiliate marketing strategy.

Finding the Right Fit for Your Website or Blog

One of the most important things you can do as an affiliate marketer is to find the right fit for your website or blog. This means finding products or services that align with your niche and will appeal to your audience. Here are some tips to help you find the right fit for your website or blog:

1. Know your audience: The first step in finding the right fit is to understand your audience. Who are they? What are their interests? What problems do they have that you can solve? Once you have a clear understanding of your audience, you can start looking for products or services that will appeal to them.

2. Research products and services: Once you know your audience, you can start researching products and services that will appeal to them.

Look for products or services that are relevant to your niche and that your audience is likely to be interested in.

3. Check out affiliate programs: Once you've found products or services that you're interested in promoting, check out the affiliate programs that they offer. Look for programs that offer competitive commissions and that are easy to sign up for.

4. Read reviews: Before you start promoting a product or service, read reviews from other affiliates. This will give you an idea of what to expect and will help you avoid any potential pitfalls.

5. Test and track: Once you've found a product or service that you want to promote, start testing and tracking your results. Use analytics tools to track clicks, conversions, and sales. This will help you optimize your campaigns and make sure you're getting the best possible results.

By following these tips, you can find the right fit for your website or blog and start earning commissions as an affiliate marketer. Remember, it's all about finding products or services that your audience will love and that will help you achieve your affiliate marketing goals.

Chapter 3 – Build a Website or Blog

- **Why having a website or blog is important for Affiliate Marketing**
- **Choosing the right platform and domain name for Affiliate Marketing**
- **Designing a building your site for Affiliate Marketing**

Why having a website or blog is important for affiliate marketing.

If you're new to affiliate marketing, you may be wondering whether you really need a website or blog to be successful. The short answer is yes, you absolutely do. Here's why:

1. A website or blog gives you a platform to promote your affiliate products.

One of the key benefits of having a website or blog is that it gives you a place to showcase your affiliate products. You can create detailed reviews, how-to guides, and other types of content that help your audience understand the benefits of the products you're promoting. This can help you build trust with your readers and increase the likelihood that they'll make a purchase through your affiliate link.

2. A website or blog makes it easier for people to find you.

When you have a website or blog, you have a presence on the internet that people can find through search engines, social media, and other channels. This makes it easier for potential customers to discover you and learn about the products you're promoting. Without a website or blog, you're limiting your ability to reach a wider audience.

3. A website or blog helps you establish yourself as an expert in your niche.

When you create high-quality content on your website or blog, you're demonstrating your expertise in your niche. This can help you build a following of loyal readers who trust your recommendations and are more likely to purchase products through your affiliate links. Over time, this can lead to higher earnings and more success as an affiliate marketer.

4. A website or blog allows you to track your progress and improve your strategy.

When you have a website or blog, you have access to analytics tools that can help you track your progress and see what's working and what's not. This can help you identify areas where you need to improve your affiliate marketing strategy and make adjustments to optimize your results.

In short, having a website or blog is absolutely essential for affiliate marketing success. It gives you a platform to promote your affiliate products and establish yourself as an expert in your niche, while also making it easier for people to find you and track your progress over time. So if you're serious about becoming a successful affiliate marketer, start by building your own website or blog today.

Choosing the Right Platform and Domain Name for Affiliate Marketing

If you're new to affiliate marketing, one of the first things you need to do is choose the right platform and domain name. This can be overwhelming, but with a little research and planning, you can set yourself up for success.

Choosing a Platform

There are many platforms to choose from when it comes to affiliate marketing. Some of the most popular include:

1) Blogging Platforms: These platforms include WordPress, Tumblr, and Blogger. They are great for creating content and building an audience.

2) Social Media Platforms: Social media platforms like Facebook, Instagram, Twitter, and Pinterest can be used to promote affiliate products. They're great for building a following and engaging with your audience.

3) E-commerce Platforms: Platforms like Amazon, eBay, and Etsy allow you to sell products directly to customers. You can also promote affiliate products on these platforms.

Choosing a Domain Name

Once you've chosen a platform, it's time to choose a domain name. Your domain name should be memorable, easy to spell, and easy to pronounce. Here are a few tips to keep in mind when choosing a domain name:

1) Keep it short and sweet: The shorter your domain name, the easier it is to remember.

2) **Make it easy to spell:** Avoid using complex words or unusual spellings that could confuse people.

3) **Use keywords:** Including keywords in your domain name can help with search engine optimization (SEO).

4) **Avoid hyphens and numbers:** These can make your domain name more difficult to remember and can look unprofessional.

5) **Make it Brandable:** Your domain name should be unique enough to stand out and memorable enough to be associated with your brand

Conclusion

Choosing the right platform and domain name is an important first step in affiliate marketing. Take your time, do your research, and choose a platform and domain name that aligns with your goals and target audience.

With the right platform and domain name, you'll be well on your way to building a successful affiliate marketing business.

Designing and Building Your Site for Affiliate Marketing

Affiliate marketing is an excellent way to monetize your website or blog. But before you can start making money through affiliate marketing, you need to have a website that is designed and built to attract and convert customers. In this chapter, we'll explore the key elements of designing and building a website for affiliate marketing.

1. Determine Your Niche (This has been mentioned several times)

The first step in designing and building your website is to determine your niche. By now you should have an idea of what niche you would like to get involved in. What topic or industry do you want to focus on?

 The more focused your niche, the easier it will be to attract a specific audience that is interested in your products or services.

2. Choose the Right Platform

Next, you need to choose the right platform for your website.

There are many website builders and content management systems available, but some of the most popular include WordPress, Squarespace, and Wix.

Choose a platform that is user-friendly, easy to customize, and offers the features you need to run an effective affiliate marketing program.

3. Create a Responsive Design

A responsive design is essential for any website that wants to attract and retain visitors.

A responsive design means that your website will adjust to different screen sizes, making it easy for visitors to navigate and read your content on any device.

This is particularly important since a lot of people will be browsing your site on their mobile devices.

4. Use High-Quality Images and Videos

In order to attract and engage visitors, you need to use high-quality images and videos on your website. This will help to showcase your products and services in the best possible light. Make sure your images and videos are clear, sharp, and professional-looking.

5. Focus on User Experience

The user experience on your website is critical to its success. You need to make it easy for visitors to find what they're looking for and navigate your site without frustration. This means designing clear navigation menus, using readable fonts and colors, and providing easy-to-understand content.

6. Optimize Your Site for SEO

Search engine optimization (SEO) is essential for any website that wants to attract organic traffic from search engines like Google. SEO involves optimizing your website with targeted keywords, creating quality content, and building high-quality links to your website.

7. Include Calls-to-Action

Finally, you need to include calls-to-action (CTAs) on your website. CTAs are specific instructions that encourage visitors to take action, such as clicking on a link or making a purchase.

These CTAs should be prominently displayed on your website and should be designed to grab the visitor's attention.

By following these tips, you can design and build a website that is optimized for affiliate marketing and ready to attract customers and generate revenue.

Chapter 4 – Creating Quality Content

- Why Creating Quality Content is Essential for Affiliate Marketing
- Types of content that work best for affiliate marketing.
- Tips for creating engaging content that drives traffic and conversions.

Why Creating Quality Content is Essential for Affiliate Marketing

Creating Quality Content is the backbone of a successful affiliate marketing strategy. As an affiliate marketer, your goal is to provide value to your readers and encourage them to purchase the products or services that you promote. Your content plays a crucial role in this process, as it helps you build trust with your audience, establish yourself as an authority in your niche, and ultimately increase your affiliate sales.

When it comes to creating quality content, there are a few key things to keep in mind. First and foremost, your content should be informative, engaging, and relevant to your target audience. This means that you need to understand your audience's pain points, interests, and needs, and tailor your content accordingly.

In addition to being informative and engaging, your content should also be well-written and visually appealing. This means using proper grammar and spelling, breaking up text with subheadings and bullet points, and incorporating high-quality images and videos.

Finally, your content should be optimized for search engines. This means using relevant keywords in your content and metadata, creating compelling headlines and meta descriptions, and linking to other high-quality content on your website.

By creating quality content that meets these criteria, you'll be able to attract more traffic to your website, engage with your audience, and increase your affiliate sales. So if you're serious about success in affiliate marketing, make quality content creation a top priority.

Here are some benefits to creating quality content:

1. Good content attracts more traffic: People are always looking for high-quality content online,

and if you can provide it, they'll come to you. This means more traffic to your website, which in turn leads to more sales.

2. Builds trust with your audience: When you create high-quality content, you're showing your audience that you're an expert in your field. This builds trust and credibility, which makes it more likely that they'll buy from you.

3. Improves your search engine rankings: Search engines love high-quality content, so if you can create it, you'll likely see an improvement in your search engine rankings. This means even more traffic and sales for your business.

4. Increases engagement: Quality content is more likely to be shared and engaged with by your audience, which means even more exposure for your business.

Overall, creating quality content is essential for affiliate marketing success. Not only does it

attract more traffic to your website, but it also builds trust, improves your search engine rankings, and increases engagement with your audience. So if you want to succeed as an affiliate marketer, don't skimp on the content!

Types of content that work best for affiliate marketing.

When it comes to affiliate marketing, the type of content you create can have a big impact on your success. Here are a few types of content that tend to work well for affiliate marketing:

1. Product Reviews: Writing detailed reviews of products that you're promoting can be a great way to provide value to your audience and encourage them to make a purchase. Be sure to highlight both the pros and cons of the product so that readers feel like they're getting an honest assessment.

How to Write Product Reviews that Convert

If you're looking to create content that drives sales, writing product reviews is a great place to start. But not all product reviews are created equal. To really make an impact and convert your readers into customers, you need to follow a few key guidelines.

- Be Honest: First and foremost, you need to be honest in your product reviews. If you're not, your readers will quickly see through it and lose trust in your content. Be transparent about any flaws or downsides to the product, as well as any positives.

- Be Specific: The more specific you can be in your product reviews, the better. Don't just say that a product is "good" or "bad." Give specific examples of why you feel that way. For example, if you're reviewing a camera, talk about the quality of the images, the ease of use, and any standout features.

- Use Visuals: Whenever possible, include visuals in your product reviews. This can be photos of the product, screenshots of the user interface, or even videos of you using the product. Visuals help to break up the text and make the review more engaging.

- Provide Comparisons: One of the most helpful things you can do in a product review is to provide comparisons to other products in the same category. This helps readers understand how the product stacks up against the competition and can also help them make a decision on which product to buy.

- Include a Call to Action: Finally, make sure to include a call to action at the end of your product reviews. This could be a link to buy the product, a coupon code, or a sign-up form for a newsletter. The goal is to convert your readers into customers, so don't be afraid to be direct in your CTAs.

By following these guidelines, you can create product reviews that are not only informative but also effective at driving sales and conversions.

2. Tutorials and How-To Guides: If you're promoting a product that requires some know-how to use, creating tutorials and how-to guides can be a great way to provide value to your readers and encourage them to make a purchase.

3. Comparison Articles: Comparing different products within the same niche can be a great way to help your readers make an informed decision about which product to buy. Be sure to highlight the strengths and weaknesses of each product to help readers make a decision.

4. Gift Guides: Creating gift guides around certain holidays or special occasions can be a great way to promote specific products and earn commissions. Be sure to provide value by suggesting products that your readers will actually be interested in.

5. Video Content: Creating video content around the products you're promoting can be a great way to engage your audience and encourage them to make a purchase. Consider creating product demos, tutorials, or other types of video content that show off the product in action.

No matter what type of content you create, be sure to provide value to your audience and make it clear why they should consider purchasing the product you're promoting. With the right approach, affiliate marketing can be a great way to earn commissions while helping your readers find products they'll love.

Tips for creating engaging content that drives traffic and conversions.

1. Know Your Target Audience: Understanding your audience is key to creating content that resonates with them. Research and identify their preferences, interests, and pain points.

2. Create a Catchy Headline: A compelling headline is the first thing that grabs the reader's attention. It should be clear, concise, and promise value.

3. Use Visuals: Including visuals such as images, infographics, and videos can make your content more engaging and easier to understand.

4. Keep it Simple: Avoid using complex jargon or industry-specific terms that your audience may not understand. Make your content easy to read and digestible.

5. Tell a Story: Stories have the power to evoke emotions and connect with readers on a deeper level. Incorporate storytelling techniques to make your content more relatable.

6. Offer Solutions: Provide actionable tips and solutions that your audience can implement to solve their problems or improve their lives.

7. Encourage Engagement: Encourage your readers to engage with your content by asking questions, inviting them to share their opinions, and responding to their comments.

By following these tips, you can create quality content that not only drives traffic but also converts readers into customers or loyal followers.

Chapter 5 – Build an Email List

- Why Building an email list if Important for Affiliate Marketing
- How to build an email list from scratch
- Email marketing strategies for Affiliate Marketers

Why Building an Email List is Important for Affiliate Marketing

As we've discussed in previous chapters, affiliate marketing can be a highly effective way to earn money online. But if you're serious about making a sustainable income as an affiliate marketer, building an email list is absolutely essential. Here's why:

1. Email marketing is still one of the most effective ways to reach your audience.

Despite the rise of social media and other digital marketing channels, email marketing remains one of the most effective ways to reach potential customers. With an email list, you have a direct and personalized way to communicate with your audience.

2. It allows you to build a relationship with your audience.

When people sign up for your email list, they're giving you permission to contact them directly.

This means you have an opportunity to build a relationship with them over time, providing them with helpful information and building trust. When they're ready to make a purchase, they're more likely to turn to you as a trusted source.

3. You can promote relevant products to your subscribers.

By segmenting your email list and sending targeted messages, you can promote relevant products to your subscribers. This means you're more likely to make sales, since your subscribers are already interested in the types of products you're promoting.

4. It's a great way to keep your audience engaged.

With regular email newsletters and updates, you can keep your audience engaged and interested in what you have to say. This means they're more likely to keep coming back to your website or blog, and more likely to make a purchase when you do promote a product.

5. You own your email list.

Unlike social media followers or website traffic, your email list is something you own and control. This means you're not at the mercy of changing algorithms or other factors that could impact your reach. As long as you're providing value to your subscribers, you'll have a direct way to reach them for years to come.

In short, building an email list is one of the most important things you can do as an affiliate marketer. By doing so, you'll have a direct way to reach your audience, build trust and credibility, and promote relevant products to people who are already interested in what you have to offer.

How to Build an Email List from Scratch

If you're just starting out in the world of email marketing, building an email list from scratch can feel like a daunting task. But fear not—there are plenty of strategies you can use to grow your list and start engaging with your subscribers.

Step 1: Create a Lead Magnet

A lead magnet is an incentive that you offer to potential subscribers in exchange for their email address. It can be anything from a free e-book to a discount code to a video tutorial. The key is to make sure that your lead magnet is valuable and relevant to your target audience.

Step 2: Create a Landing Page

Once you've created your lead magnet, it's time to create a landing page where people can sign up to receive it. Your landing page should be simple, clean, and focused on the benefits of your lead magnet. Make sure to include a clear call-to-action (CTA) that tells people what they'll get when they sign up.

Step 3: Promote Your Landing Page

Now that you've created your lead magnet and landing page, it's time to start promoting them. There are many ways to do this, including:

- Social media: Share your landing page on your social media channels and encourage your followers to sign up.

- Blogging: Write blog posts that are related to your lead magnet and include a CTA at the end of each post.

- Paid advertising: Consider investing in paid advertising on platforms like Facebook or Google to reach a wider audience.

Step 4: Optimize Your Opt-In Forms

Opt-in forms are the forms that people fill out to sign up for your email list. Make sure that your opt-in forms are easy to find and use. Consider using pop-up forms, slide-in forms, or exit-intent forms to capture more leads.

Step 5: Follow Up with Your Subscribers

Once you've started building your email list, it's important to follow up with your subscribers on a regular basis. Send them valuable content, promotions, and updates to keep them engaged and interested in your brand.

In conclusion, building an email list from scratch takes time and effort, but it's an essential part of any successful email marketing strategy. By following these steps and staying consistent, you'll be well on your way to growing your list

and building strong relationships with your subscribers.

Email Marketing Strategies for Affiliate Marketers

Email marketing is one of the most powerful tools that affiliate marketers have at their disposal. By building a targeted email list and sending out regular emails with affiliate offers and promotions, you can generate a steady stream of commissions and sales. However, email marketing is also one of the most competitive digital marketing channels, with consumers inundated with hundreds of emails every day. To stand out from the crowd and maximize your results, you need to have a strategic approach to email marketing. In this section, we'll cover some of the most effective email marketing strategies for affiliate marketers.

Segment Your Email List

One of the most important things you can do to improve the effectiveness of your email marketing is to segment your email list. This means dividing your email list into different groups based on various criteria, such as demographics, interests, and behavior. By doing this, you can tailor your emails to each group's specific needs and interests, increasing the chances that they will engage with your emails and take action.

Personalize Your Emails

Personalization is another critical element of successful email marketing. Instead of sending generic emails to your entire list, you should use personalization to make your emails more relevant and engaging. This could include using the recipient's name in the subject line or adding product recommendations based on their interests or past purchases.

Use Attention-Grabbing Subject Lines

Your subject line is the first thing your subscribers see when they receive your email. If it doesn't grab their attention, they're likely to delete your email without even opening it. To maximize your open rates, invest time in crafting attention-grabbing subject lines that pique curiosity or offer a clear benefit.

Provide Value in Every Email

Every email you send should provide value to your subscribers. Whether it's providing helpful information, offering a discount or promotion, or sharing exclusive content, you should always aim to provide something that your subscribers will find valuable. This not only helps build trust and credibility with your subscribers but also increases the chances that they will take action on your offers.

Include a Clear Call-to-Action

Finally, every email should include a strong call-to-action (CTA) that encourages subscribers to take action. This could be anything from clicking a link to visiting your website to making a purchase. Your CTA should be clear, concise, and easy to follow, so make sure to include a prominent button or link that stands out from the rest of your email.

Conclusion

Email marketing is a powerful tool for affiliate marketers, but it requires a strategic approach to deliver the best results. By segmenting your email list, personalizing your emails, using attention-grabbing subject lines, providing value, and including a clear call-to-action, you can maximize the effectiveness of your email marketing campaigns. So why not start implementing these strategies into your next email marketing campaign and watch your affiliate commissions soar?

Chapter 6 – Promoting Your Affiliate Links

- How to promote your Affiliate Links Effectively
- Using Social Media to Promote your Affiliate Links
- Other Ways to Promote Your Affiliate Links

How to promote your affiliate links effectively

Affiliate marketing can be a lucrative way to earn money online, but it's not as simple as simply signing up for a program and waiting for the money to roll in. To succeed as an affiliate marketer, you need to know how to promote your affiliate links effectively. In this section, we'll cover some of the most effective ways to do just that.

1. Build a website or blog

One of the best ways to promote your affiliate links is by creating a website or blog. This allows you to establish a personal brand and build an audience that trusts your recommendations. When creating your site, be sure to focus on a specific niche so that your content is targeted and relevant to your audience.

2. Use social media

Social media platforms like Facebook, Twitter, and Instagram can be great places to promote your affiliate links. You can share links to your website or blog, as well as directly to affiliate products. Be sure to use compelling images and engaging captions to grab your audience's attention.

3. Create engaging content

Whether you're writing blog posts, creating videos, or recording podcasts, it's important to create engaging content that draws people in and keeps them coming back for more. Share your personal experiences with the products you're promoting and be honest and transparent about your affiliations.

4. Offer incentives

Offering incentives like discounts, free products, or exclusive content can be a great way to entice people to click on your affiliate links. You can also use these incentives to build your email list and establish a direct line of communication with your audience.

5. Collaborate with other influencers

Collaborating with other influencers in your niche can help you reach new audiences and build your credibility. You can write guest posts for other blogs, participate in joint webinars or podcasts, or even create a joint product or service.

By following these tips, you can effectively promote your affiliate links and start earning money online. Remember, it takes time and effort to build a successful affiliate marketing business, so be patient and stay focused on your goals.

Using Social Media to Promote Your Affiliate Links

Social media has become a powerful tool for marketers looking to promote their products and services. And if you're an affiliate marketer, social media can be a great way to drive traffic to your affiliate links and earn commissions.

Here are a few tips for using social media to promote your affiliate links:

1. Choose the right social media platforms

Not all social media platforms are created equal when it comes to promoting affiliate links. Some platforms, like Facebook and Instagram, have strict rules about affiliate marketing and may even ban or penalize users who violate their guidelines. Other platforms, like Twitter and Pinterest, are more affiliate-friendly and can be great places to share your links.

2. Be transparent about your affiliate links

It's important to be transparent with your followers about the fact that you're using affiliate links. This helps build trust with your audience and ensures that you're complying with FTC guidelines. Be upfront about the fact that you're earning a commission when someone clicks on your link or makes a purchase.

3. Create compelling content

To promote your affiliate links on social media, you need to create content that captures your audience's attention and encourages them to click on your links. This could be anything from product reviews to tutorials to sponsored posts. Whatever type of content you create, make sure it's high-quality and engaging.

4. Use hashtags

Hashtags are a great way to increase the visibility of your social media posts and make them more discoverable. When you're promoting your affiliate links, use relevant hashtags that will help your target audience find your content.

5. Build relationships with your followers

Finally, remember that social media is all about building relationships. Take the time to engage with your followers, respond to their comments and questions, and show them that you're a real person who cares about their needs. By building a loyal following, you'll be able to promote your affiliate links more effectively and earn more commissions in the long run.

Other Ways to Promote Your Affiliate Links

In addition to the traditional ways of promoting your affiliate links such as blogging, social media, and email marketing, there are many other ways to get your links in front of potential customers. Here are some creative ways to promote your affiliate links:

1. Guest Post on Other Blogs

Guest posting on other blogs can be a great way to get your affiliate links in front of new audiences. Find blogs in your niche that accept guest posts, and offer to write a post that includes your affiliate links.

2. YouTube Videos

Creating YouTube videos is a great way to promote your affiliate links. You can create videos that review products, share tutorials, or offer other helpful information, and include your affiliate links in the video description or as annotations within the video.

3. Paid Advertising

Paid advertising can be an effective way to promote your affiliate links, especially if you have a larger budget. You can use Google AdWords, Facebook Ads, or other advertising platforms to target specific audiences and drive traffic to your affiliate links.

4. Webinars

Hosting webinars is a great way to educate potential customers about products and services related to your affiliate links. You can offer valuable information and advice and include your affiliate links in your presentation or in follow-up emails to attendees.

5. Product Reviews

Writing product reviews can be a great way to promote your affiliate links. Offer honest, detailed reviews of products related to your niche, and include your affiliate links in the review.

6. Coupon Sites

There are many coupon sites that allow you to share discount codes and coupons for products and services related to your affiliate links. Share your codes on these sites to attract new customers and drive traffic to your affiliate links.

In conclusion, there are many creative ways to promote your affiliate links beyond the traditional methods. With a little creativity and some hard work, you can increase your affiliate sales and earn more commissions.

Chapter 7 – Tracking your Results.

- **Why tracking your results is important for affiliate marketing.**
- **How to track your results using analytics tools.**
- **Analyzing your results and making adjustments.**

Why tracking your results is important for affiliate marketing.

One of the most critical aspects of affiliate marketing is tracking your results. Without proper tracking, it's difficult to know what's working and what's not. Here are a few reasons why tracking your results is so essential in affiliate marketing.

1. It helps you identify which campaigns are performing well.

Tracking your results allows you to see which of your campaigns are generating the most traffic and conversions. This information is crucial because it helps you focus your efforts on the campaigns that are most effective, rather than wasting time and resources on those that aren't.

2. It helps you optimize your campaigns for better results.

Once you've identified which campaigns are performing well, you can use that information to optimize your campaigns for even better results. For example, you might tweak your ad copy or landing page to improve your conversion rate.

3. It helps you spot trends over time.

Tracking your results over time allows you to spot trends and identify patterns. For example, you might notice that certain campaigns tend to perform better during certain times of the year. This information can help you plan your campaigns more strategically and take advantage of seasonal trends.

4. It helps you measure your return on investment (ROI).

Ultimately, tracking your results allows you to measure your ROI. By knowing how much you're spending on each campaign and how much revenue you're generating, you can determine whether your efforts are yielding a positive ROI. This information is critical to making informed decisions about where to invest your time and resources.

In conclusion, tracking your results is an essential part of affiliate marketing. It allows you to identify which campaigns are performing well, optimize your campaigns for better results, spot trends over time, and measure your ROI. If you're not already tracking your results, now is the time to start!

How to track your results using analytics tools

One of the most important aspects of any marketing campaign is tracking your results. Without data, it is difficult to know if your efforts are paying off or if adjustments need to be made. Fortunately, there are many analytics tools available that can help you track your results and make informed decisions about your marketing strategy.

1. Define your goals

Before you start tracking your results, it is important to define your goals. What are you trying to achieve with your marketing campaign? Do you want to increase website traffic, generate leads, or boost sales? Once you have defined your goals, you can start tracking the metrics that matter most.

2. Choose your analytics tool

There are many analytics tools available, but the most popular tool is Google Analytics. Google Analytics is a free tool that provides a wealth of information about your website traffic, including where your visitors are coming from, how long they stay on your site, and what pages they visit. Other popular analytics tools include SEMrush, Moz, and Ahrefs.

3. Set up your account

Once you have chosen your analytics tool, you will need to set up your account. This typically involves adding a tracking code to your website. If you are using Google Analytics, you can set up your account by creating a Google account and linking it to your website.

4. Track your metrics

Once your account is set up, you can start tracking your metrics. Some of the most important metrics to track include website traffic, bounce rate, goal conversions, and revenue. These metrics can help you determine what is working and what is not, and help you make informed decisions about your marketing strategy.

5. Analyze your data

Once you have collected data, it is important to analyze it. This involves looking at trends over time and identifying patterns that can help you improve your marketing strategy. For example, if you notice that a particular landing page has a high bounce rate, you may need to make adjustments to improve the user experience.

6. Make adjustments

Based on your analysis, you may need to make adjustments to your marketing strategy. This could involve tweaking your landing pages, adjusting your ad targeting, or changing your messaging. By making data-driven decisions, you can optimize your marketing strategy for success.

In conclusion, tracking your results using analytics tools is an essential part of any marketing campaign. By defining your goals, choosing the right analytics tool, tracking your metrics, analyzing your data, and making adjustments, you can optimize your marketing strategy and achieve your goals.

Analyzing Your Results and Making Adjustments

Once you've implemented your marketing strategy, it's important to take a step back and analyze the results. This will help you determine what's working and what's not, so that you can make adjustments to your approach. Here are some steps to follow when analyzing your results:

1. Start with your goals. What were you hoping to achieve with your marketing strategy? Did you want to increase website traffic, generate more leads, or boost sales? Look at your data to see if you're meeting those goals.

2. Evaluate your metrics. What metrics are you tracking? Look at things like website traffic, bounce rate, time spent on site, conversion rate, and social media engagement. Are those metrics moving in the right direction? If not, why not?

3. Identify areas for improvement. Based on your analysis, identify areas of your marketing strategy that need improvement. Look for trends in your data, and try to pinpoint the root cause of any issues.

4. Make adjustments. Once you've identified areas for improvement, it's time to make adjustments to your marketing strategy. This might mean changing your messaging, trying new tactics, or tweaking your targeting.

5. Monitor your results. After you make adjustments, continue to monitor your data to see if those changes are having the desired effect. Be patient and give your strategy time to work, but don't be afraid to make further adjustments if necessary.

By regularly analyzing your results and making adjustments, you can ensure that your marketing strategy is always improving and delivering the best possible results.

Chapter 8 – Tips for Success

- **Common mistakes to avoid in affiliate marketing**
- **Tips for staying motivated and avoiding burnout**
- **How to scale your affiliate marketing business**

Common mistakes to avoid in affiliate marketing

Affiliate marketing can be a lucrative business, but like any other business, there are some common mistakes that you should be aware of before getting started. In this chapter, we'll take a look at some of the most common mistakes made by affiliate marketers and how to avoid them.

Mistake #1: Choosing the wrong products to promote.

One of the biggest mistakes that affiliate marketers make is choosing the wrong products to promote. It's important to choose products that are relevant to your audience and that you truly believe in. If you're promoting products that you don't genuinely believe in, your audience will see right through you and you won't earn their trust.

Mistake #2: Not diversifying your income streams.

Relying on one affiliate program or one product to generate all of your income is a recipe for disaster. Instead, you should diversify your income streams by promoting multiple products and using multiple affiliate programs. This will help to protect you from fluctuations in the market and ensure that you always have multiple streams of income coming in.

Mistake #3: Not tracking your results.

Tracking your results is essential to success in affiliate marketing. If you're not tracking your results, you won't know what's working and what's not. This means that you could be wasting time and money on ineffective strategies. Make sure to track your results using analytics tools so that you can see which strategies are working and which ones need to be tweaked.

Mistake #4: Not building an email list.

Building an email list is one of the most important things you can do as an affiliate marketer. Your email list is a direct line of communication with your audience, which means that you can promote products and services to them directly. This is much more effective than relying on social media or other platforms to reach your audience.

Mistake #5: Not providing value.

Finally, one of the biggest mistakes that affiliate marketers make is not providing value to their audience. If you're constantly promoting products without providing any real value, your audience will quickly lose interest in what you have to say. Make sure to provide valuable content and resources to your audience on a regular basis, even if it's not directly related to the products you're promoting.

In conclusion, affiliate marketing can be a fantastic way to earn a living online. However, it's important to avoid these common mistakes if you want to be successful. By choosing the right products, diversifying your income streams,

tracking your results, building an email list, and providing value to your audience, you can set yourself up for long-term success as an affiliate marketer.

Tips for staying motivated and avoiding burnout

Motivation is a key factor in achieving success. When you're motivated, you're more likely to stay focused, work hard, and reach your goals. However, staying motivated can be easier said than done, especially when you're working on a long-term project or goal. It's easy to get burned out and lose motivation, which can make it difficult to keep moving forward. Here are some tips for staying motivated and avoiding burnout:

1. Set realistic goals: One of the biggest reasons people lose motivation is because they set unrealistic goals. When you set goals that are too lofty or impossible to achieve, it can be demotivating. Instead, set smaller, achievable goals that you can work toward every day.

2. Find inspiration: Inspiration can come from many different sources, whether it's a mentor, a

book, or a motivational speaker. Find someone or something that inspires you and use it to keep yourself motivated and moving forward.

3. Take breaks: It's important to take breaks to avoid burnout. Take a 10-15 minute break every hour or so to stretch, walk around, or do something that relaxes you. This will help you stay fresh and focused.

4. Stay organized: When you're working on a long-term project or goal, it's important to stay organized. Keep a to-do list and prioritize your tasks. This will help you stay on track and avoid feeling overwhelmed.

5. Celebrate small victories: Celebrating small victories is a great way to stay motivated. When you reach a milestone, take a moment to celebrate your accomplishment. This will help you stay positive and motivated as you work toward your larger goals.

6. Surround yourself with positivity: Surrounding yourself with positive people and influences can help you stay motivated and focused. Seek out people who inspire you and avoid negative people who bring you down.

7. Exercise and Eat Healthy: Exercise and eating healthy are important for staying motivated and avoiding burnout. Exercise can help you reduce stress and improve your mood. Eating healthy can also improve your mood and give you the energy you need to stay motivated.

8. Mix things up: Doing the same thing every day can get boring and lead to burnout. Mix things up by trying something new or taking on a new challenge. This will keep things interesting and help you stay motivated.

By following these tips, you can stay motivated and avoid burnout as you work toward your goals. Remember, motivation is key to success, so don't give up!

How to Scale Your Affiliate Marketing Business

Scaling your affiliate marketing business is crucial if you want to take your earnings to the next level. Here are some tips to help you do just that:

1. **Diversify Your Affiliate Programs:** Don't rely on just one affiliate program. Join several programs and promote a variety of products to maximize your earning potential.

2. **Stay Up-to-Date with Industry Trends:** Affiliate marketing is a constantly evolving industry. Stay on top of the latest trends and developments to make sure you're not falling behind.

3. **Build a Strong Brand:** Building a strong brand helps you stand out from the competition and establishes trust with your audience. Invest time and effort into creating a strong brand identity.

4. Create Valuable Content: Providing valuable content to your audience is key to building a loyal following. Focus on creating high-quality content that provides value to your readers.

5. Leverage Social Media: Social media is a powerful tool for promoting your affiliate products. Build a strong presence on social media platforms and use them to drive traffic to your website.

6. Use Paid Advertising: Paid advertising can be a highly effective way to scale your affiliate marketing business. Use platforms like Google Ads and Facebook Ads to reach a wider audience.

7. Automate Your Processes: As your business grows, you'll need to find ways to streamline your processes. Look for ways to automate tasks like email marketing and social media management to free up more time for other tasks.

By following these tips, you can take your affiliate marketing business to the next level and achieve even greater success.

Chapter 9 – Next Steps and Resources

- Where to go for more information and support
- Tools and Resources for Affiliate Marketers
- Next Steps for building a successful affiliate marketing business

Where to go for More Information and Support

Affiliate marketing can be a challenging field to navigate, and it's normal to feel overwhelmed at times.

Fortunately, there are plenty of resources available to help you learn more, stay up-to-date on the latest trends and techniques, and connect with others in the industry.

Here are a few places to go for more information and support:

1. Industry conferences and events: Attending conferences and events can be a great way to meet other affiliate marketers, learn from industry experts, and stay up-to-date on the latest trends.

Some popular events include Affiliate Summit, Affiliate World, and Affiliate Marketing Days.

2. Online forums and communities: There are countless online forums and communities dedicated to affiliate marketing, where you can connect with other marketers, ask questions, and share advice. Some popular forums include Warrior Forum, Digital Point, and AffiliateFix.

3. Blogs and podcasts: There are many blogs and podcasts dedicated to affiliate marketing, where you can learn about the latest trends, get tips and advice, and hear from experts in the industry. Some popular blogs include Affiliate Marketing Blog, AM Navigator, and AffiliateTip. Popular podcasts include the Affiliate Buzz and the Affiliate Guy Daily.

4. Affiliate networks: Affiliate networks are a great source of information and support, as they often provide resources, training, and support to their affiliates. Some popular affiliate networks include ShareASale, Commission Junction, and Rakuten Marketing.

5. Affiliate marketing courses: If you're looking for more structured learning, there are many online courses and training programs available that can teach you the ins and outs of affiliate marketing. Some popular courses include Affilorama, Wealthy Affiliate, and ClickBank University.

One of the best platforms that I know of for Affiliate Marketing is a platform called Wealthy Affiliate. I have been a member of this platform for 4 years and I have learned a ton of things about affiliate marketing.

Here are a few reasons that I would encourage you to take a look at the wealthy affiliate platform.

Wealthy Affiliate is a top-rated platform for affiliate marketing training, website building, and online business development.

What sets Wealthy Affiliate apart is its comprehensive approach to teaching its members how to build and grow successful online businesses.

With Wealthy Affiliate, you get access to an extensive library of training materials, tools, and resources that cover everything from website design and content creation to SEO and PPC advertising. Additionally, the Wealthy Affiliate community is incredibly supportive, with members always willing to offer advice, feedback, and encouragement.

Whether you're a complete beginner or an experienced marketer, Wealthy Affiliate is an excellent choice for anyone looking to gain tips, techniques, and resources to build a profitable online business.

- Wealthy Affiliate is the leading platform for successful internet businesses worldwide.

• Their innovative approach to affiliate marketing propels the industry forward with unique tools and resources.

• Wealthy Affiliate provides a complete package of education, training, and support for internet entrepreneurs.

• Over 50,000 independent authority bloggers have chosen Wealthy Affiliate as their go-to platform for internet marketing.

No matter where you go for support and information, the key is to stay curious and keep learning. Affiliate marketing is a constantly-evolving field, and the more you know, the better equipped you'll be to succeed.

Tools and resources for affiliate marketers

Affiliate marketing can be a great way to earn money online, but it's not always easy to know where to start.

Fortunately, there are many tools and resources available to help affiliate marketers succeed. One of the most important resources is a good affiliate network, which can connect you with advertisers and help you find products to promote.

Other valuable tools include analytics software to track your performance, keyword research tools to help you optimize your content for search engines, and social media management tools to help you promote your content and engage with your audience.

(Please refer to our resource section for a suggested list of analytics software, keyword research tool and social media management tools.)

Additionally, there are many online communities and forums where affiliate marketers can share tips and advice, network with other professionals, and stay up-to-date on industry news and trends.

As I mentioned earlier in the book, you can join our Affiliate Marketing network of over 2.1 billion people for FREE.

You will get a ton of resources to get your started in Affiliate Marketing such as:

- 1 FREE website or blog
- 10 Affiliate Marketing bootcamp videos
- 30 Free keyword searches
-

With the right tools and resources, anyone can become a successful affiliate marketer.

Next steps for building a successful affiliate marketing business.

Building a successful affiliate marketing business takes time, effort, and a solid plan. Once you've gotten started with the basics, it's important to focus on a few key next steps to take your business to the next level. One important step is to constantly test and optimize your marketing strategies to ensure that you're getting the best possible results.

This might involve changing up your website design, testing different calls to action, or experimenting with different types of content. Another important step is to build relationships with your audience and your affiliate partners. This might involve creating engaging content that resonates with your audience, or reaching out to potential partners to build mutually beneficial relationships.

Finally, it's important to stay up-to-date with the latest trends and developments in the affiliate marketing industry, and to constantly keep learning and growing so that your business can continue to thrive.

Chapter 10 – Legal and Ethical Considerations

- Understanding and Complying with FTC guidelines
- How to disclose Affiliate Relationships Properly
- Know Your Rights and Responsibilities as an Affiliate Marketer

Understanding and Complying with FTC Guidelines

As an affiliate marketer, it's important to understand and comply with the Federal Trade Commission (FTC) guidelines. These guidelines are in place to protect consumers and ensure transparency in advertising. Failure to comply with the guidelines can result in fines and legal action. Here are some key points to keep in mind:

1. Disclose Your Affiliate Relationship: It's important to disclose your relationship with the company you are promoting. This can be done through a disclaimer on your website or in your social media posts. The disclosure should be clear and easy to understand.

2. Be Honest: Be honest in your product reviews and recommendations. Don't exaggerate the benefits of a product or make false claims.

Misleading consumers can lead to lost trust and credibility.

3. Disclose Affiliate Links: Any links that lead to products or services that you are promoting should be disclosed as affiliate links. This lets consumers know that you will receive a commission if they make a purchase.

4. Use Clear and Concise Language: Use language that is easy to understand and avoid technical jargon. This makes it easier for consumers to understand what they are getting into.

5. Keep Up-to-Date: Stay up-to-date with the latest FTC guidelines. The guidelines can change over time, so it's important to stay informed.

By following these guidelines, you can build a solid reputation as an affiliate marketer and maintain trust with your audience. Remember, honesty and transparency are key in the world of affiliate marketing.

How to Disclose Affiliate Relationships Properly

As an affiliate marketer, it's important to disclose your relationship with the products and services you promote. Not only is it required by law in many countries, but it's also an ethical way to build trust with your audience. In this chapter, we'll discuss how to disclose your affiliate relationships properly to stay compliant and transparent with your audience.

What is Affiliate Disclosure?

Affiliate disclosure is a statement or notice that informs your audience that you may receive compensation for promoting or recommending certain products or services. This compensation can be in the form of commissions, referral fees, or other rewards. Affiliate disclosure is required by law in the US, UK, Canada, and many other countries to prevent deceptive advertising and ensure transparency in online marketing.

Why is Affiliate Disclosure Important?

Affiliate disclosure is important for several reasons:

- It's a legal requirement in many countries to disclose affiliate relationships.

- It builds trust with your audience by being transparent about your financial interests.

- It helps you avoid potential legal issues and penalties for non-disclosure.

- It sets a good example for other affiliate marketers and promotes ethical marketing practices.

Ways to Disclose Affiliate Relationships Properly

1. Use clear and conspicuous language

Your disclosure statement should be easy to read and understand for your audience. Use clear and concise language that explains your relationship with the products or services you promote. Avoid jargon or technical terms that may confuse your readers.

2. Place the disclosure in a prominent location

Your disclosure statement should be in a prominent location on your website or blog. It should be visible to your readers before they make a purchase or take any action related to the promoted product or service. A good location for the disclosure is near the beginning of your post or near the affiliate link.

3. Use different formats for disclosure

You can use different formats to disclose your affiliate relationships, such as text, images, or videos. However, the disclosure should be clear and conspicuous regardless of the format you use. For example, you can use a banner or badge that says "Affiliate Disclosure" or "Sponsored Content" to indicate that you may receive compensation.

4. Disclose affiliate relationships on each post

Your disclosure statement should be included in every post that contains affiliate links or promotions. This ensures that your readers are aware of your relationship with the promoted products or services, even if they access your content through different channels.

Conclusion

Disclosing your affiliate relationships properly is an essential part of affiliate marketing for beginners. It helps you build trust with your audience, comply with legal requirements, and promote ethical marketing practices. By following the best practices, we discussed in this

chapter, you can ensure that your affiliate disclosure is clear, conspicuous, and compliant with the laws and regulations in your country.

Knowing Your Rights and Responsibilities as an Affiliate Marketer

As an affiliate marketer, it's important to know your rights and responsibilities when it comes to promoting products and earning commissions. By understanding the rules and regulations surrounding affiliate marketing, you can avoid costly mistakes and build a successful business. Here are some key points to keep in mind:

Your Responsibilities as an Affiliate Marketer

As an affiliate marketer, you have a responsibility to promote products ethically and legally. This means:

- Disclosing your affiliate relationship: You must disclose your relationship with the merchant when promoting products. This can be done by including a disclaimer on your website or in your social media posts.

- **Promoting products honestly:** You should only promote products that you believe in and that you think will benefit your audience. Don't promote products just because you'll earn a commission.

- **Following the merchant's rules:** Each merchant has their own rules and guidelines for their affiliate program. Be sure to read and follow these rules to avoid getting kicked out of the program.

Your Rights as an Affiliate Marketer

As an affiliate marketer, you have certain rights when it comes to the affiliate program. These include:

- **Access to tracking and reporting:** The merchant should provide you with access to tracking and reporting tools so that you can see how well your promotions are performing and how much money you're earning.

- **Timely payments:** The merchant should pay you on time and in accordance with the terms of the affiliate program.

- **Fair treatment:** The merchant should treat all affiliates fairly and not show preference to certain affiliates over others.

Conclusion

Knowing your rights and responsibilities as an affiliate marketer is essential for building a successful business. By following the rules and guidelines set out by the merchant and promoting products ethically and legally, you can earn commissions and build a loyal audience.

Don't forget to disclose your affiliate relationship and only promote products that you believe in to maintain your credibility as an affiliate marketer.

Resources

Resources for Affiliate Marketing – I am an affiliate of some of these platforms and will get a commission if you choose to use my link.

*Represents that I am an Affiliate

FREE access to my Digital Marketing Course
https://pastordre.com/free

FREE download of the Affiliate Marketing for Beginners Audio Book
https://pastordre.com/audio-book

*FREE website and blog –
https://PastorDre.com/siterubix

*Free Membership to our Affiliate Marketing Training and Resource Platform –
https://www.pastordre.com/wealthyaffiliate

*Social Media Automation –
https://pastordre.com/automation

Thank you.

If you have any questions, please reach out to me at pastordre@pastordre.com

Thank you.

If you have any questions, please reach out to me at

Made in the USA
Monee, IL
22 September 2023